RIDING TOP DECK

JOHN WRIGHT
(AKA **Doublé Dekker**)

APS PUBLICATIONS

About the Author
Doublé (*pronounced Doo-Blay*) **Dekker** was born in Edinburgh, Scotland, moved to Birmingham in the early 90's and has remained here ever since.

APS Books,
4 Oakleigh Road,
Stourbridge,
West Midlands,
DY8 2JX

APS Books is a subsidiary of
the APS Publications imprint

www.andrewsparke.com

First published worldwide by APS Books in 2019

A catalogue record for this book is available from the British
Library

ISBN 9781789960181

Acknowledgments

This collection of mostly doggerel poems was inspired by, and helped take the boredom out of, my daily commute to work. I hope it helps bring a smile to those who may recognise some of the scenarios described.
I would like to thank all the people of Birmingham who travel on the buses daily for helping to spark moments of joy and inspiration in my life.
Needless to say all characters appearing in this work are fictitious. Any resemblance to real persons, living or dead is purely coincidental.

{Note: the poem, *Drunken Bus Home*, was previously published in "Birmingham Bound" by the Book Club Brum.}

LIGHTER POEMS

Sorry not in service

I wish I lived at 'Sorry not in Service'.
For through the night and day,
Buses rush past eagerly,
Heading out that way.

They come in both directions,
Hurtling through the streets,
Quite frantic to get out there -
Are they served with treats?

I wish I lived at 'Sorry not in Service'
Cause I'd never need to wait,
For even the plenteous fifty,
Cannot match their rate.

They must have special bus stops
And be special people too,
For every bus that I see
Contains but the basic crew.

These are not common people,
Who ride the 'Sorry' bus,
But special 'royal' dignitaries,
Who wish to make no fuss.

Oh how I long to live at, 'Sorry not in service',
Or even to live nearby.
To see it once, then perish,
What a perfect way to die!

Bus Drivers

The buses, the buses,
The early morning rushes.
The curses, the pushes,
The heart stopping flushes.
Who feels the pain?
Who takes the strain?
The driver, the driver, that's who!

The driver. The driver.
The rush hour survivor,
The ducker and diver,
The race-car admirer.
The driver, the driver, that's who!

The government adviser,
The dole bound skiver,
The biker, the hiker,
The penny-pinching miser,
Will, at sometime in their life,
(Maybe with their wife)
Get on a bus,
Without any fuss,
And then marvel at their choice,
As they rejoice with one voice,
At their double-decker saviour,
(With impeccable behaviour).
The driver, the driver, that's who!

The in-and-out weaver,
The bus-lane believer,
The traffic-light deceiver,
The one true geezer,
The driver, the driver, that's who!

In the main, we all gain,

Because they take our pain,
All our stress and distress,
As they weave without panic,
Through the never ending traffic,
They're terrific,
And prolific,
When the queues are horrific.
For its they who take the strain.

Through the sunshine,
through the rain,
Bus drivers everywhere,
Are taking great care
To ensure they get us there!

So who should we cheer?

The driver. The driver.
The rush hour survivor,
The ducker and diver,
The race-car admirer.
The driver, the driver, that's who!

The in and out weaver,
The bus-lane believer,
The traffic-light deceiver,
The one true geezer,
The driver, the driver that's who!

Drunken bus home

A little too much of the grape juice,
And too many jugs of hop,
I lurch, with Chinese food in hand,
Towards the waiting stop.

Apologising as I go,
Knowing what we all well know,
That eating or drinking on the bus
Is a serious no, no, no!

Hot curry sauce, runs down my chin,
And stains my office shirt,
What once was white and pristine,
Now looks like rain-soaked dirt.

(Or is it that blob from Gorbachov's brow,
Or a classic Rorschach blot?
Or something from deep in my psyche,
Something I never forgot?)

The Spring roll turns to winter,
As it sags into the foil,
And grains of rice slip through my hands,
To die on a foreign soil.

The 35 bursts into sight,
Bumping its pot-holed way,
From the bustling heart of the City,
And the bridge below Queensway.

The bin accepts my refuse,
As I stagger slowly aboard,
Swaying down the crowded aisle
While the bus rejoins the road.

Down Pershore Street we bundle,
Like a pin-ball ricochet,
My trail of Chinese debris,
Recedes as we drive away.

A little too much of the grape juice,
Has addled my spinning brain,
Tonight I'll sleep like a baby
Tomorrow, that hangover pain.

The bus keeps running regardless,
Of behaviour that seems like a slight,
As it turns its back at the corner,
On one more drunk in the night.

Trafffic

Are there three F's in traffic?
The driver seems certain there are.

"Look at that f-ing traffic,
Who do they think they are?
That f-ing truck
can go to fff...
And as for that f-ing car!!!"

There must be three f's in traffic,
For the driver swears there are!

Habit

Old Abe, from the ground floor flat,
Who had a stroke last September
Used to work in Cotteridge,
About 4 miles away.
[A two-bus journey.]

We often used to catch the 6.38 together
Then he vanished for a while.
That was when he had his stroke.
After that, they changed the nature of his job.
And now he only works three days a week,
And doesn't start 'til nine,
 And it's only in Kings Heath,

About half-a-mile away,
A one-bus journey!
[Or a 15 minute walk!]
But,
on the days he does work,
He still gets the 6.38.
Gets off in Kings Heath,
Gets on the 50 to go further up the street,
[A two-bus journey.]
And sits in a café
Next to his new workplace until 5 to 9.

Habit, the repeating pattern in all our activity,
That makes us slave to its demands.

But, as he says, he's never been late for work!

Reading books purchased on Kindle on the Bus
– a warning!

Nourishing the mind
on the mindless journey to work
I bought some poetry books from Kindle
to help while away the time.

The
Last book of poems
Had
For reasons I could not fathom
No
Particular
Theme
 To it.
And one particular poet seemed intent on breaking
Up
Her lines of
verse
In an
Odd (perverse)
Stilted
Fashion
That made no sense.

So much
for a
RELAXING
edifying
JOURNEY

to work!

To man on the bus who had been overgenerous with his deodorant.

Go easy with the 'Lynx', man.
It's us who smell the stinks, man.
The blast on the back of the throat, man;
The esophagus coughagus, gasp, man;
The rasps and grasps. The gassed. Man.
Go easy with the 'Lynx', man.
We don't want to be extinct, man
Go easy with the 'Lynx'.

The Trouble with Kindle

The trouble with Kindle is
That you can no longer impress
By how thick the book is!

Schoolboys

Back on the back of the bus meanwhile
Two schoolboys share a smile
The seat in front has chewing gum
To stick to someone's bum!

Deviation from route

People are sitting comfortably
The bus is speeding on,
The hectic week is over,
The stress is almost gone.

Faces relaxed and smiling,
Body language, "slumped",
The strain of 'keeping up the show',
Has gone - all pretence dumped.

But then, for some strange reason,
We fail to make a turn
And unannounced, we're speeding on,
The mood becomes concern.

Where are we speeding off to?
This is not the route?
Scared unspoken questions,
In anxious minds take root.

Are we being driven forcibly,
To some dark distant land?
And will we need a Stanley,
To come and shake our hand?

People rise to leave the bus,
Thinking they mistook
The bus' destination
The number and the route.

The drive drives relentlessly,
In unrepentant mode,
Not prepared to share with us
The secrets of the road;

Or why we are now heading,
Off to Bordesly Green,
When we should be in Moseley
Or nearer Acocks Green.

Panic grips the passengers
Some rise up from their seats,
As we proceed at greater speed
Down unfamiliar streets.

Someone accosts the driver,
"You're off the usual route!"
Some words are heard in answer,
For me: too soft, too mute.

Then unofficial whispers
Hiss snake-like down the bus,
As people share their knowledge
Wrapped up in a cuss.

Human communication,
Is a mystery I know,
But couldn't the driver warn us,
Tell us before we go,

That the road is blocked at Highgate,
That a new route has been found;
That there will be deviation
But the way around's quite sound,

Then all these work-worn people,
Would not have had this pain,
Knowing the bus would deviate
But resume the route again?

It's a common human foible
To fear what is unknown,

From the meaning of the universe,
To our nightly journey home.

Let's not over complicate
That which is not so,
Please tell us before we board the bus,
The route that you must go.

Then we can sit oblivious
To the twists and turns of fate,
Knowing we'll get there sometime,
Though running a little late.

Who to sit next to?

Who to sit next to
Is always a bind;
Sometimes it's really just
"Take what you find."

But sometimes you learn
That you do have a choice
You can make your own future
You can use your own voice.

Like that pair in the garden
Who – defying god –
Chose apples, not chastity,
How most, very odd.

Why did they do it?
To get under his skin?
To tease the old codger?
To piss in his wind?

Why did they do it?
Was it just to annoy?
Or did that fine kingdom
They seek to destroy?

To question authority?
To challenge his might?
To exert their own freedom
Their own puny right?

Or was it just lust,
In that serpent-like guise,
Who poisoned their thinking,
Poured scorn in their eyes?

No matter its myth-tory[1]
Not our concern,
We've got judgments colossal
To challenge our brain.

So on this rare occasion
On boarding that bus
That great god in heaven,
Without any fuss

Had given me options
The choice where to sit,
My one crack at freedom
I have to admit.

I start scanning the faces
The pretty one's first
Cause I'm thinking of apples
In truth its plain lust.

With failure on that front,
Then someone who's clean:
A business man – suited -
A housewife serene.

Or maybe that schoolboy
From that posh private school,
At least he won't smell
Like the jabbering fool

Whose loud talking mobile,
And beer can in hand,
Marks him a no, no,
A clear no-man's-land.

---

[1] *Combination of Mystery and History.*

At last, quite exhausted,
Still tender and raw,
I've made my decision,
From judgment and law.

I must stand by my choice,
Be it perfect or flawed.
This master has chosen
I've raised my own voice.

I have shown I'm a man
By making a choice.
I bite into the apple,
As I plonk on a seat,
To journey: in victory?
joy? or defeat?

Week 14th -21st January 2012 – No Poem

The bus is grave-yard quiet.
People sit hunched and huddled,
Wrapped up in themselves,
And their warm, winter clothing.
It's too cold to move,
Too bitter to breathe,
Too raw to talk.
Even the chatty mobiles have succumbed to the cold,
Snug in their owner's pocket or purse.
The whirring noise of the heater
Breaks the silence,
With its frigid promise of hope;
Blowing cold air round the bus.
In my brain
Thought processes have shut down:
Too numb even for a poem.

Waiting

In the early morning frost
Three buses stood restless on Priory Queensway
Waiting on their appointed departure time,
Coughing and wheezing like tubercular babies.

Upper Deck

breathing our last
the funereal silence of the upper deck
echoed in the steamed up windows

Steamed up windows

For most the steamed up window is addressed
by drawing the hand backwards across the glass
in a few mechanical motions;
like the fan of the windscreen wiper
or maybe the tracks of a royal wave.
But here,
sitting before me on top deck of the bus,
was a man on the front seat
who had taken the time
and the trouble
to clear a perfect rectangle
 with which to see the oncoming world,
framing his head perfectly
from behind
like a miniature TV.

The Ghost of Druids Heath

For those that ride the 50
Late night out of town,
One sight you never want to see,
Is the Druid, dressed in brown.

A ghastly brown, a ghostly brown,
A brown that shines and glows,
That glistens in the headlights,
As the driver brakes and slows.

Sometimes it glides right through the bus,
Cursing through its teeth,
Those who left him bleeding
On the stones of Druids Heath.

There's very few can see him,
But we all know when he's there:
That mood of desperation,
That tension in the air.

That empty can that suddenly,
Comes rattling down the stairs,
That icy blast that swirls and spins,
And bristles all your hairs.

The sense that someone's watching you
From another time and place,
The sense that something's out there,
Some thing your eyes can't trace.

It sometimes stays a stop or two,
Two stops, but barely three,
Then muffled screeches rend the air,
And the bus emerges free.

And those who ride the 50
Late night out of town,
Never forget their meeting
With the Druid dressed in brown.

Fervently *(After Billy Collins)*
(Advice for aspiring novelists - eliminate adverbs!)

I waited fervently for the bus.

Well,
possibly not,
'fervently'.
I wasn't really waiting in an intensely passionate or ardent
manner.

But,
nevertheless, I was certainly keen for it to come.

And,
having waited 30 minutes for a 10 minute service,
I was decidedly getting passionate about its non-arrival.

But, yes,
have to agree,
hardly ardent,
hardly intensely enthusiastic,
or even experiencing a burning passion for it to arrive,
Just quietly fuming in that most understated English way.

The boy, the bus and the bladder

It was the day the Mayan's predicted the end of the world,
And I'd waited in until after eleven - just in case.

Catching the late running 76 to the gym
I noticed that the whole world seemed to be on the road
We crawled along at a glacial pace
up roads we'd normally speed down.
No matter
 I was in no rush.
Because downstairs was so full I'd gone upstairs
where, surprisingly, there were only three other people:
An old man sat near the front,
two teenage boys on the back seat
heads down playing with their mobile phones
and me – plonking down somewhere near the middle of the bus
for aesthetic reasons of balance.
The boys were lively, speaking in loud excited voices,
doing a word-perfect rap rendition
of a song they were listening to
then impersonating a high squeaky voiced character
no doubt from some TV or video show
performing together in perfect harmony.
Their conversation ranged widely and randomly
from rap songs to the gay boy called Grant.
Also,
we now knew that one of the boys was desperate for a pee.
They were concocting some plan for him to pee behind the
back seat,
then out the window
but it was all too much for the cross-legged boy
he just couldn't go.
By now we had lurched and lumbered
and been tossed around and thrown roughly about
for almost ten uncomfortable minutes
As the driver strove to make up time.

Finally we turned slowly and hesitantly into a long
Christmas- shopping generated line of traffic
stretching back to the top of Cartland Road.
It was here the boy had his epiphany
and the challenge was thrown down.
Because we were moving so slowly
he had contrived that he would get off the bus at one stop
have a pee, and then rejoin it at bottom of the road.
"Remember and push the button to stop it", he shouted
 as his head disappeared down the stairs.
I can see the boy running
While his mate is a-chilling
And the bus it's a rolling
And his feet are turning
and his heart is churning
as he races away
Down the hill on his way
This bus is chasing
But he's still racing
The traffic is moving
But will he be grooving
and get his pee out
And will his mate shout
to have the bus stop
 at the very next stop?
He disappears from sight
at Hazelwell park
we guess what he's up to
steaming up the grass
feeling the relief as that
hot warm pee
runs from his body
like a slurping lover's kiss
or a cup of hot tea.
But just as we're waiting
the traffic is breaking
the lights have turned

we're rushing and we're shaking
making a break
for the bottom of the hill.
Will he make it?
just shake it,
 come on boy don't flake it
The bus is moving
and you ain't in sight!
they he rejoins the pavement
Making a statement
his challenge is in play
he's well on his way
his mate is ecstatic
the boy's doing magic
he's beaten the bus at his game.
As we stop at the stop
his heart is pounding
But his bladder is empty
And his triumph is resounding.
His mate has erupted
in giggles of laughter
the boy's got his pee,
it was just what he was after.
They slump back in their seats
ecstatic and emphatic
from their action dramatic.
The rest of their day
must surely go their way
after such daring
after such sharing
after all that effort
to have a simple pee.

By the way, the world didn't end,
It just got wetter.

Shared anxiety

The anxiety was almost palpable
As he sat looking at his watch
The young man in fashionable rust-red trousers.
Who constantly sought reference points on the passing
landscape.
His panic spread through the bus.
Eventually the call came
'Yes, we're still stuck in traffic.
I think another 15 mins.
Yeah. Yeah."
Now the legs started going.
Jiggling up and down
it looked as if he was anxious for the toilet -
couldn't hold it in.
But that was not it at all.
That was clearly not it at all.
The bus grew jittery with his panic.
The girl next to me began to steal furtive glances at him
twisting the bracelet on her arm
frantically as she did so.
The old man in the seat in front
began to look at his watch
even more often than the boy.
I squirmed uncomfortably in my seat, unable to sit still.
Yes, we were all getting it
as if by osmosis
his anxiety was transmitting itself down the bus.
We lumbered on stopping at every stop
as unnecessary people got on for short-hop trips,
or schoolgirls held us up
 while they giggled inanely trying to find their passes.
The whole mood of the bus was fraught.
Would he get there in time?
15 minutes passed.
Then the unexpected call at least 20 stops out.

"Hi, yes,
we're only a few stops away from town now"
he lied.
Concluding,
"See you soon."
muttered under his breath as if wishful thinking.
On Highgate Middle Way
he got up and proceeded down the bus
only to stand near the disabled seat
shifting from leg to leg
as if his bladder was approaching bursting point,
but it was not that at all
That was clearly not it at all.
We lumbered slowly down Bradford Street

As if in slow motion,
He, meanwhile, was mentally pulling his hair out!
At last we reached the market where we stopped.

The last I saw of him
was a streak of rusty red trousers
heading past the fruit-laden stalls
in the direction of New Street.
My pulse went down.
Relaxing we turned the corner into Moor Street
and I got off the bus.

Bus Reality

"You need a reality check, boy!"
She announced loudly from the back of the bus,
Then, as if it needed emphasizing, added,
"You seriously need a reality check boy!"

Sitting near the front,
 I mused on what that might actually mean?
Was she suggesting he question his ontological views?
Were, in her opinion, his metaphysics askew?

Had his speculations on Epistemology
Strayed beyond realistic expectations,
With reference to its limits and validity?
Or had he merely mixed up and confused
His haecceity and his quiddity?

Maybe she was exhorting him to consider Calderon's view
That 'Life is but a Dream'
And all is not what it might seem?

Or was she having a dig at his behaviour,
And had he failed to obey Kant's categorical imperative?
(Although we have too little evidence
To constructively pursue this narrative.)

I wondered too,
If his Weltanschauung had become so perverse,
That everything she thought
He thought the obverse?

But then again
It was maybe very simple.
Did she, in a moment of startling insight,
Really just mean,
That he wasn't going to be getting into her knickers tonight?

SOBER POEMS

Daily Drudge

From my house
the number 50 bus
carries me over the river Styx
to my work;
where, each day,
I die a little.

Devil daughter/family curse
Sanity, Madness and the Family.[2]

The Mother, some seats away,
Lashed out at the daughter – aged eight –
With such venom and hate
That the startled bus of Brummies shed
Silent tears of sorrow and of pain,
At the fairy-tale darkness of her madness
Reading like a tale from Esterson and Laing.
The ugly horrid, hatred that
Flowed out from her tongue
Was shocking to behold:
Like a devil, unrepentant and bold,
Being cast out of hell
To manifest again on earth.
To take root here and fester
For one more score of years
Until the daughter, in her own cyclic,
Predetermined way,
Would bequeath this quick nightmare of terror
To her own offspring,
And send them on their own cosmic carousel
Tortured and screaming
Spiraling towards eternity,
From which they could never leap
Unless they were willing to dive,
And swim naked and vulnerable,
Through a sea of love and blood
Until all the wretched actions of their past
Had been altered one by one,
Transformed and burned,
In the bright blue flames of truth.

---

[2] *Sanity, Madness and the Family, by Laing and Esterson (1964).*

The Letter

That morning, I was waiting at the stop,
To make my way
To see a friend. But first I meant to drop
In and have some breakfast at the café.
The 11 came - as always - running late.
I scrambled on, and sitting at the back,
My thoughts began to wander to the food.
I saw before me, heaped upon my plate,
An egg filled roll, atop a little stack,
Of pancakes caked in syrup: 'Looking good'!

I chilled a little, shifted in my seat,
I checked my phone,
Then, leaning back and stretching out my feet,
I slid into my bus-mode comfort zone.
I glanced around, surveyed the bustling bus,
Full of eager people on their way,
To some elicit meeting - furtive sex?
Or just their daily shopping, with no fuss.
Others, on some outing for the day,
With reasons, no doubt simple, or complex.

At last I see them, sitting on their own,
The frail old pair.
Their pain is theirs, and clearly theirs alone,
As into blank despair, they sit and stare.
Their backs towards the driver, gazing out,
They watch their future pass, after it's been.
Unsure of where they're heading, where they're bound.
Intrigued, I watch intently as they flout,
The normal type of conduct that is seen,
Intent instead, to nurse their painful wound.

She gripped the letter tightly in her hand.
It's fairly clear,

Its content's bleak; its message never planned.
Headlong into a world of woe and fear
This news has plunged them. Seeking for relief,
They only have each other now, they know.
The impact on their world has been profound!
They traveled on in silence with their grief.
Putting on this outward, brave-faced show,
While inside, screams of terror drown all sound.

She fretted every second of that trip.
Her fingers touched
And played discordant tunes upon her lip.
As if that act could ease the truth she clutched,
Within the damning letter on her lap.
He stared, like someone struck, and deep in shock,
Unable to make sense of what he felt,
And turned and turned again his woolen cap.
There were no words, no impetus to talk,
To analyse the cards they had been dealt.

Her thick tweed coat was old and tired and worn,
It's black and white,
And rough, entangled wool, unfashionable and torn.
Their drab attire spoke loudly to their plight
As he, in grey, anonymous and poor,
Announced, in muted terms, their working class,
And all the disadvantage that had brought:
Their failing health; the illness with no cure;
Those endless years of worry and distress,
And every penny counted, each moment fraught,

With wondering if more would ever come.
And unemployment
Knocking on their door, and this the sum,
The total of their life's accomplishment:
A formal, printed letter, breaking news,
Objectively, unfeelingly and brusque,

That all, within their temple is not well.
Just one more battle they are set to lose.
This tragedy, both comic and grotesque,
Presented here on earth, but straight from hell.

They sit with eyes fixed firmly to the floor.
In Oak Tree Lane,
A surge of people rise and crowd the door.
The hospital rekindles those in pain.
The couple stand, their arms are interlocked,
And shuffling in the queue they wait their turn.
She takes the lead, and 'mother' now becomes;
To guide him, like a shepherd does his flock.
And stepping down, they go at last to learn,
Accept and deal with, face what trouble comes.

The bus moved on. I'd lost my appetite.
My journey now
Divest of joy, seemed hollow, flat and trite.
It's clear there's very little we can know,
We live our lives haphazardly and wild,
And even those who plan, and have some goal,
Can never guarantee a sure result.
We travelled on; no sign exhorted 'Yield'!
No 'Satnav' giving guidance on our role,
Just suffering, our basic life default.

Random ruminations

The day starts early waiting in the rain,
Just two or three brave souls on shifting feet,
 Moving to dispel or dull the pain.

With quick perfunctory nod we grunt and greet,
And gaze downhill in hope to see the bus,
But nothing moves; no motion shakes the street.

Someone decries the rain with little fuss,
We add our sense of outrage and despair,
Rounding off this ritual with a cuss.

Again we look; again the street is bare,
Then someone moves, a lumbering sight is seen.
We all relax, our sighs massage the air.

An orange streetlight bounces off the screen,
And turns the coloured livery to black,
Merging with the darkness of this scene.

Too late now, to turn our heel and walk,
The strange ungainly motion of the bus,
His fixed us here, defined our forward track.

No time to argue cause, nor to discuss,
To question; raise a doubt, or intervene,
We're swept along in Time's relentless thrust.

We file on board. This well rehearsed routine,
Will see us all locate a private space:
An act of self-defence, or just pure mean?

We little care our actions lack all grace,
For once on board, we gave shape to the lie,
And don with ease, our work resilient face.

Raindrops fall from brollies shaken dry,
And soak the slippy floor, but leave no mark,
Our rain-resistant shoes will walk on by.

We reach the high street, here I disembark,
And huddle in the shelter to stay dry,
While others, sail on out into the dark.

With this twice-daily ritual we comply,
This hour-long journey made with little fuss,
Resented though, but never questioned why?

Is this the case? And are we really thus?
Do we succumb so easily, and live,
A life of subjugation to some boss;

To blindly work: enact the nine-to-five,
Accept constraints upon our hopes and dreams,
And kill at source the joy of being alive?

These questions go unanswered, for it seems,
We'd rather abdicate all sense of choice,
And blandly fit into precast regimes.

The fifty comes, I still this nagging voice
And step on board. My doubts remain behind
Still trapped in Torpor's life-destroying vice.

I climb the stairs and sit, to calm my mind.
The man in front I've seen on other days,
He too has made his god the daily grind.

His orange workman's trouser's bright display,
Counteract the fact that life is hard,
Carved undisguised into his face of grey.

His daily toil all sense of joy has marred,

Dulled his youthful vision, robbed his hope,
And by his failed ambitions he's been scarred.

He leans forward. (A deferential slope?)
Then sits so still and motionless, he seems,
Fully lost in thought. Is this his means to cope?

Across from me a youth is lost in dreams,
His unseen iPod plugged into his ears,
Bobbing slowly to a stream of rhythmic themes.

His hoodie up, the colour so last years,
That bright cerulean blue that lit our streets,
And shone through riots; fueled irrational fears,

And now sits here, a needful source of heat.
Bright beneficence lights this moody gloom,
And signs the cross; a blessing on these seats.

Or so it seems, so radiant is its plume.
We bathe in its penumbra, happy souls,
"Take us now oh lord, prepare our tomb!"

Our words rise up unheard, our heavenly goals
Frustrated one more time; and so we fall,
Assuming once again our mundane roles.

As human beings we err, not one, but all,
Because we only see a partial truth.
Our lives are bound, our visions frail and small.

So quickly gone the ideals of our youth,
We must be kind, and selfless in our acts,
For doing so can keep our journey smooth,

Avoiding all the pitfalls that can tax,
A man who stumbles blindly through this world

And has no guide to point to fruitful tracks.

I look across, and see the youth is curled,
His legs too tall for these tight, stuffy seats.
He stares ahead, his life as yet unfurled,

But looking in his eyes I sense defeat,
Too many battles so far have been lost,
No glorious forward charge, just base retreat.

We reach the town. Our journey ends at last,
The rain still falling heavy from the skies.
We shuffle off. Our paths in life have crossed,

And may well cross again. There is no prize,
No goal, no great reward, we walk away.
To work. To dull routine. Don our disguise,
And with that last deceit, we greet the day.

Winter
Sestina for the season

The dark is but a symbol of the mood
That wraps the season up in clothes of gloom.
We stand apart. The bus stop, cold and wet.
No word is said, no sound but rain is heard.
We shuffle in the sharp and cutting wind.
The bus arrives, and numb we climb inside.

Like automatons – lifeless, dead inside,
Our thoughts subdued, as if a distant mood,
Hovered like a ghost upon the wind,
And blew its smoky shadows through our gloom.
No thought of joy, no note of hope is heard.
We stand or sit alone, dull and drab and wet.

Submariners, we dive through streets of wet,
The crush of pressure, tangible inside,
Where silent screams of pain pass by unheard.
The season numbs us all, and taints our mood,
As we, warped up in ugly clothes of gloom,
Draw dark collars closed, against the wind.

The doors and windows sealed, but yet the wind,
Finds ways to show our weakness, prove us wet,
As steamed up glass intensifies our gloom.
Osmosis spreads this view to all inside,
Who feel the shifting currents of this mood
Permeate their thoughts with no word heard.

Are we but bovine creatures in some herd
With other hapless souls forever twinned
Our bleak communications dully mooed?
Or is there hope, some joy that yet may whet
Our appetite for life, and from inside,

Release the spell to thus dispel our gloom?

Or are we weak, and wallow in our gloom
Deny all hope, denounce solutions heard,
Give reasons why no greatness lies inside,
And never taste the chance that fresh new winds,
Blow towards us with the cold and wet,
Preferring to surrender to our mood?

A mood of gloom and meekness, such a mood,
That guts our inside, leaves us weak and wet,
And blows unheard dead leaves in winter's wind.

Tales from the Top Deck

I

Old Madge McFadyen took her rightful place,
The long back seat, atop the twenty bus.
From here she held her court, and sealed the fate,
Of all that lived, and breathed; each creed, each race.
To her, the art of judgement caused no fuss,
Just simple right and wrong, and love and hate.
Within an instant she'd deliberate,
No facts required, no evidence, no proof,
Just her assured conviction of the truth:
The sentence passed: no pardon, no debate.

II

Three husbands buried, and the fourth in toe,
Old Madam 'M' was never known as slow.
Her ragged mind made tales the whole day long,
To judge those whom she saw - keep moral law.
Her judgements often came as revelation,
To those who failed to gain her approbation.
(To many, though, they just seemed downright wrong!)
Detractors spoke in whispers of her flaw,
Her tongue of gossip, heart corrupt with hate.
For Madam 'M' there was no such debate.

III

Munroe his name, a bin-man for the Council,
Sat innocently gazing through the glass.
But Mrs 'M' knew better. He was trouble!
Mass-murderer! His spare time steeped in blood.
The bodies buried in the knee-high grass,
Behind the Council tip, face down in mud.

(Gasp!)

Some said, that Mr Munroe once complained,

That Madge McFadyen's bins were over-filled.
But this vile lie could never be sustained,
(He'd filled her bin, with limbs from those he'd killed.)

IV

Those homosexual boys, who flaunt their sex,
Caused apoplectic pain to Mrs 'M',
- A childless mother with a heart of gold -
Who all her life had valued procreation.
They'd giggle at some filthy obscene text,
Effeminate and floppy, brash and bold,
And cause her blood to boil, her tongue to spit,
To curse, to rant, and into Hell condemn,
Each freak of nature, slight against creation,
And watch them roast forever in Hell's pit.

V

He sat un-phased, demeanour smooth as silk.
The Devil worship, palpably upon him;
His hair of feathers; blood below his nails,
His skin, as pale, and frail, as fresh skimmed milk.
She shifted in her seat, and saw the flood,
As red grab-bars flowed fountains of fresh blood,
To distant cries - his dying victim's wails.
The youth got up to leave, his eyes were grim.
Myopic Madge McFadyen sighed relief,
And cursed this stranger's strange, uncouth, belief.

Bus Rap

Well,
I got up on the bus
And I flash my pass
But the driver gets heavy
Dissing my ass.
Wants to see it again
As if it ain't gen.

This sense of suspicion,
Is boiling my brain.
The younger generation
Demoted again.

Just cause I'm young
And I got a lippy tongue
Don't mean I'm a crook
or a gun toting gangsta.

Who am I? What am I?
Well to me I'm justa kid
Who's trying to get rid
Of this mistrusting frustration.
I'm climbing up the ladder
Trying to get an education.
But I'm taken for a ride,
- Contemplating suicide -
Cause this feeling inside
Is impossible to hide
You dis me
dismiss me
putting me down
ain't no way
to make me come around.

And I think I'm gonna cuss
Cause of all this fuss
there's a sense of disgust
and I aint got it sussed.
So, "Hey bus driver
I aint no fare skiver.
Keep your eyes on the road
And reign in your hate
My pass is up-to-date
But your bus is running late!"

Exact Copy

From the top of the bus
I observe the world we pass.

A cafe advertises "Instant coffee".
A printing shop boasts "Exact Copy".

As the bus trundles on,
I struggle with the oxymoron.

Surely an inexact copy
Is not a copy at all?

Fresh (Haiku)

Bright sunlit morning.
I open all the windows.
Empty bus, cool, fresh.

Smelly

A dancing blue fog – a cartoon fart -
Surrounded the drunk,
Lying at the back of the bus.
A discarded banana-skin of sprawled out limbs,
Flopped listlessly across three tarnished seats.

The air was rancid with his smell:
Unwashed clothes, dirt-stained flesh,
Tobacco breath, and stale, day-old alcohol,
Intertwined with the early scent of death!

Involuntary retching convulsed the bus,
Forcing down the body's natural defences.
Gasped breaths through gritted teeth,
Distended nostrils flared in red reaction.
No windows open.

Control!

Politeness forbids a response.

Then,

Small breaths taken guardedly through the nose,
While faces smile to camouflage their pain.
A cheap deflection from the fetid truth.

In a hazy awareness of the Bus' discomfort
His hands fan away a putrid fart,
As he draws out a can of shoddy deodorant
And sprays the air around his splayed out form.

In despair, I rise,
Unwilling to perpetuate the pretence further,
And exit from the bus.

Breathing in sigh after sigh of relief,
As fresh untarnished air, replenishes my lungs.

Breathing

I sat alone on the top deck of the bus.
('Deck' from ships I wondered?)
The windows were closed
And, as more and more people boarded
the steam from our breaths increased.
Soon the windows were misted over
not uniformly at first, but slowly, gradually.
Eventually,
every window succumbed.
The view had been lost to the steam.

In cases like this, one often wonders if one should open a
window
but then that seems like a defiant act
so one sits still
breathing in the rancid air
and realising just how much our lives are part of each other
as the breath from the man behind me
mingled in my lungs with the breath
from the girl at the front of the bus.
How interlinked we all are

INDEX

VERSE FROM APS PUBLICATIONS
(www.andrewsparke.com)

Broken English (Andrew Sparke)
Fractured Time (Andrew Sparke)
Gutter Verse & The Baboon Concerto (Andrew Sparke)
Love & Levity (Andrew Sparke)
Refracted Light (Andrew Sparke)
Silent Melodies (Andrew Sparke)
Tea Among Kiwis (Andrew Sparke)
Tequila & Me (Andrew Sparke)
The Mother Lode (Andrew Sparke)
Vital Nonsense (Andrew Sparke)
Wicked Virtue (Andrew Sparke)
Close But Not Close Enough (Lee Benson)
Every Picture Hides A Friend (Lee Benson)
Failing To Be Serious (Lee Benson)
Jottings and Scribbles (Lee Benson)
Meandering With Intent (Lee Benson)
Random Word Trips (Lee Benson)
Riding The Top Deck (John Wright)
Shining Light Dark Matters (Ian Meacheam)
Stone People Glass Houses (Ian Meacheam)
Dub Truth (Kokumo Noxid)
Pipe Dream (Kokumo Noxid)
Fluid Edges (David Hamilton)
The Highwayman, Pink Carnations and The Re-Allocated Coal
Scuttle (Revie)
The Gathering (Malachi Smith)
Artists 4 Syria (Various)
Walking The Edge (Various)

Printed in Great Britain
by Amazon